TRUTH BY MOONLIGHT

A COLLECTION OF POEMS, PROSE, AND LYRICS

GABRIEL C. MACIEL

outskirtspress

DENVER, COLORADO

Y0-DBW-903

Truth By Moonlight
A Collection of Poems, Prose, and Lyrics

Outskirts Press, Inc.
http://www.outskirtspress.com

ISBN: 978-1-4787-6887-6

Outskirts Press and the "OP" logo are trademarks belonging to Outskirts Press, Inc.

PRINTED IN THE UNITED STATES OF AMERICA

dedicated to life,
and all the shit that comes with it.

Table of Contents

Poems and Prose

lexington and vermont

waiting for the sun to hide behind the Hollywood Hills
in this room on Lexington and Vermont that pleases me

I hear the traffic on the street and see the airplanes
in the sky
flying very close to one another
closer than I've ever seen two planes fly before
it reminds me of something that I can't quite put my
finger on
and maybe that's a good thing

the liquor store across the street made me smile
as I stared at it from the balcony of my room
freedom from myself
freedom from my stupid thoughts
only a three minute walk away

those generous gods of Los Angeles
listening to my subconscious plea
brought it to me, and just in time

thinking of the city
and of all the good times and good feelings it has
provided
thinking of the city
and of all the comfort it has given during my lowest
times

there is subtle relief hidden in the smoggy air
and in the do not disturb signs
there is subtle relief hidden in the smut stands on
the corner
and in the palm trees that line the streets

I do not know if it's enough to save me
I do not know if I'd belong or survive
but at this point
any port in a fucking storm will do

the worry in my heart

the worry in my heart
is stronger in the sunlight
when the smiling faces are
out with their lively conversations
I prefer the light from the
neon sign of my neighborhood bar
no one in there speaks of optimism
or recent travels to other countries
no one in there speaks of anything
as it should be

the worry in my heart
makes me feel foolish but not alone
because there is always
a witness to the things that we do
regardless of dark alley ways
or barbed wire fences
regardless of shadowy backstreets
or blinking street lamps
someone or something is always watching

the worry in my heart is
hollowing most of the time
but when I'm feeling bad it leaves me be
perhaps because it knows
that I no longer care
the way a lover feels when

the chaser has given up on the chase
and with the clinking of the ice cubes
that are floating in my
final cocktail of the night
my worried heart
feels a little bit better

jump

when uncertainty
takes hold
and nothing brings
calmness or comfort
everything takes a little
longer to do
even the most
mundane of tasks

so take a chance
break the cycle
of mediocrity
walk to the edge
peer into the abyss
and jump
no plan b
it makes no difference
what others say

you hear the voice
inside of you
and try as you may
to ignore it
with each passing moment
it gets a little bit louder

you know why you're here
you know your purpose
stop convincing yourself otherwise
jump
jobs will always be there
schools will always be there
your opportunity to live in a rut
will always be there
be brave
take a fucking chance
and jump

way too fast

I once was whole
but did not know it
the good times came
too easy

I once was whole
but never felt it
my laughter was
too loud

I once was whole
but could not see it
the sun was
always shining

I once was whole
but that's all over
the days flew by me
way too fast

the spiders in the trees

it's a funny thing to be alone
sometimes it's ok
but not this time
coming down from love's
relentless tug of war
I've seen and spoken to these
four walls for far too long

so let the spiders in
call them down from the trees
to devour my eyes and tongue
I don't need them anymore
let the spiders in
call them down from the trees
to feed on my imagination
I've seen and said way too much

those long happy days of summer
are finally over
and the sun has hidden somewhere
making way for the big
grey clouds to fill the sky
I know that I don't have it
in me anymore
to face that scene again

so let the spiders in
call them down from the trees
to feast upon whatever is left
why should they go hungry

songbird

distant songbird
soft and somber
through my window
you have sang
as sleeplessness
engulfs my room
like sunlight sometimes
does to rain

beneath the darkness
I have listened
to your pure
and simple song
and wondered if
you sing of something
that has gone so very wrong

I too have sorrow
that has kept me
gazing at the
pale moonlight
perhaps that's why
your song has reached me
through the hollow
dead of night

distant songbird
soft and somber
tell me what is left
for me
if you will sing
then I will listen
and my comfort
you will be

towers made of styrofoam plates

it was windy
her tower was next to mine
and I was afraid
five hundred stories tall
our towers swayed with the slightest breeze
but she didn't seem to care

I asked her "how will we get down?"
"don't worry" she said "these towers are made of
styrofoam plates."
"just remove them one at a time
until your tower is closer to the ground."

but I was paralyzed with fear
our towers swayed with the slightest movement
she didn't seem to care
she leaned across
tilting her tower closer to mine

she began removing the styrofoam plates for me
"stop it!" I screamed "my tower's shaking and yours
is tipping over!"
"we're going to die!"

she looked me in the eye
"it doesn't matter anyway."
she said
and then she jumped

I didn't see her hit the ground
the towers we'd built were too high
my tower tipped over
tossing me onto a hill
she'd pushed me toward it
leaving me on my own

I wish we'd built our towers out of stone
and not so high
they would have lasted longer

they would have stood stronger against
the wind
she wouldn't have given herself away
but now I'm here and she is somewhere
I can only hope that I'll be there too
one day

tomorrow

sometimes
when I drink too much
my dick doesn't work
I know that it's a common
problem amongst men
but it's not one that I'm
comfortable with
I'm different
at least I thought I was

how is it that I can be in a room
on a bed
with a lovely young woman
curvy
pedicured
tattooed
with a phat ass
the kind that only a brown
or black man could
truly appreciate
and not be able to get it up

spinach
kale
broccoli
carrots
these are the things that I need

but she only wants to serve me vodka
she only wants to serve me
whisky and beer and gin

I always ask for her forgiveness
she always says that it's not a problem
I tell her that tomorrow
I'm going to quit drinking
I tell her that tomorrow
I'm going to the gym
she always nods and smiles
as she pours me another

the nectar of the gods

I like to drink
although I know
I should feel bad about it
I don't
it makes me happy
and life
with all of its feelings
gives me more reasons
to drink

in good times
in bad times
the common solution, always
is to drink

if you're rich
you drink
if you're poor
you drink
if you're happy
you drink
if you're sad
you drink

drinking causes sex
drinking causes creativity
drinking causes the most

virile of men to hug and cry
drinking sometimes causes
women to make out with each other

the nectar of the gods
absolutely

segregated from the rest

I slowly walked in
through the doorway

uninvited

she did not notice me

but in her womanly way
she knew

like so many before me
I fell into her game

like a fucking fool
I gave chase
only to find myself segregated
from the rest

placed in a box
on the top shelf
of her bedroom closet

marked with the date
so that she'd never forget

now
after so much time
now
I finally feel special

my lover

my lover

so beautiful
kind
and unassuming

so gentle
sweet
and accommodating

so happy
optimistic
and full of life

my lover

so angry
sad
and crazy

so suspicious
insecure
and full of doubt

so tearful
cold
and smug

my lover

was
never like that

never

not until me

freedom's door

deliver me to freedom's door
across the sky where heroes die

the pinkish glow of souls on fire
dilutes the day with thoughts of night

embellished dreams of yesterday
remove the scars of here and now

the hazard we all live to face
will lay me down in the cold, cold earth

ancient sun burn through the fog
her grace has kept me far from sane

the time has come to dull the pain
and knock I will on freedom's door

the good ones

I often wish that I was a better writer
I imagine that the good ones
the good writers
that they can write about anything
at any time
in any place

I can only write when I'm in the mood
when my surroundings
the time of day
the music on the radio
are all just right
this fact weakens my confidence
to mount and conquer the
blank page

I imagine that the good ones
the good writers
the ones who don't suffer
the way that I do
that perhaps they don't get laid
very often
or at least as often as I do
and that this is the reason
this is why they can write about anything
at any time
in any place

and so
maybe not being one of the good ones
the good writers
the ones who can write about anything
at any time
in any place
maybe it's not such a bad thing after all

life

life
can be tricky
at times

here today
gone forever

the most important thing
is to not let it

delete you after

it's time

in solitude is where
the strong reside
there is no need for praise
there is no need for accolades
the envious criticisms of those
who wish to see you fail
fan the flames of greatness

yet there is always
a feeling of gloom
dissatisfaction
a type of emptiness
that is hard to explain

when things are good
it's there
when things are bad
it's there
a fire in the belly
when you're trying to sleep
a heavy chill in the spine
when you're trying to smile

it's time to run now
not walk
Hollywood Riviera
Bukowski Court
DeLongpre Avenue
here I come

a sweet kid

he was a sweet kid
with a sweet smile
that lit up the room
but his grandparents were too old
his aunts and uncles were too old
his cousins were too old
and he floated around unnoticed
like a ghost

he was a sweet kid
with a sweet smile
that lit up the room
but then his father died
and no one stepped in to
help raise him or show him the way
I didn't even go to the funeral

he was a sweet kid
with a sweet smile
that lit up the room
but he joined up with
the wrong crowd
and the only attention we gave
was to look down our noses at him
and to scold him

he was a sweet kid
with a sweet smile
that lit up the room
who got really mad one night
and went way too far
and the cousins
and the aunts and the uncles
still do not respond
and now
the sweet kid
with the sweet smile
that lit up the room
no longer responds, as well

a place to think

there is loud cackling laughter
at the far end of the bar

this place is normally quiet
this place is normally dark
but on this day
it's noisy
full of loud
bloated
unseemly individuals

they seem to think that everyone here
wants to listen what they have to say

it's Hollywood Blvd
but that should be no excuse
there are other places
designated places
for that type of nonsense

this bar is for the drunks
the quiet drunks
a place to think, drink
and sometimes write
in peace

but today it's full of these
most uncivilized citizens of this beloved city
they are pretending to know
the words to the songs playing
on the jukebox

but they don't know any of the words
and it is just embarrassing for all of us
fuck
now one of them is asking
to read what I'm writing
I should've drank in my room

with you again

it's been so long
since first I've seen
such madness dancing
through your eyes

as such the price
of my intent
has only been
to compromise

my prayers bled
like sounds that glide
so easily from
your bedroom door

my love
you'd never understand
nor could another
love you more

while clouds and stars
and sunny skies
delight my smiles
and drown my cries

I'll dream a dream
of you within
and fall in love
with you again

then, way back when

everyone seems to love me now
everyone wants a picture with me now
everyone tells their friends
that they know me now
everyone that knows me... now

but those who knew me then
way back when
I hardly see them
I hardly hear from them
and when I do
it's not the same
not like it was

the beauty
the wonder
the curse
of this lovely
horrible thing I've found
I don't know how to hold it
I don't know how to grasp it
to love it
or to leave it

the las vegas strip

shit faced on the
Las Vegas Strip again
4, 5, 6, 7...
who knows how many
vodka tonics I've had

good times
good friends
bright lights
broken hearts
it's better when the sun goes down

the black jack table was kind
and so was the waitress
big booze
small bill
lots of laughs

push the sofa toward the window
pour myself another
staring at the lights
of the Las Vegas Strip

she sneaks up behind me
wonders who I'm writing to
she thinks that I don't know her plan
the good times slip through my fingers
and spill onto the floor

shit faced on the
Las Vegas Strip again
good times
good friends
bright lights
broken hearts
time to add another one
to the list

just in case

feeling shitty

alone again

old timer to my left
keno machine to
my right
music playing on
the jukebox
behind me

waving at the
bartender
to no avail
thinking about
my choices
regretting my actions

love was special once
now it's just easy
I thought that was
what I wanted
once

be careful what
you wish for
just in case
you get it
the way I did

fools

typical young fool
no idea how to raise a son
no idea how to treat a son
yet he had one anyway

never taught him how to live
never taught him how to love
belittled him at every turn
to mask his own
failures and shortcomings
to mask his own
fears and insecurities

but still he wants to be praised
he believes that he is special
simply because he did not leave
simply because he stuck around

but maybe
just maybe
had he left
the kid would've been stronger
the kid would've been more independent
not so bitter and womanizing
not so fearful of anyone who
truly loved him
not so quick to burn the ones who
actually cared

typical old fool
with a son now grown
making the same mistakes that he made
causing the same heartache that he caused

the kid has become a typical old fool
himself

dream

broken shadows
bleeding hearts

the dreams undreamt
are the most tragic

embrace mistakes
and carry on

the sun
is always shining

the calm place

in the calm place
where tears find no room to form
and comfort shines
with the welcoming light
of the setting sun
thoughts of the mind are no more

no longer shackled
by the chains of reality
the soul flies free
through an eternal wilderness

all questions answered
and only regrets
laid to rest

through the withering leaves
of the autumn trees
the gentle breeze dances in my hair
buzzing all around me
like some heat maddened summer fly

the days of darkness are plentiful
yet life's rhythm beats
with an infinite pulse

born alone and left to roam
the calm place is
my only home

daytime

I dream in basic colors
the shades of the cosmos
simple
pure
and true

feet on the ground
head in the clouds
my heart dancing
somewhere in between

there's no time left
for sadness
there's no time left
for regret
there is only time left
for what is
and for what will be

not too far from where
I started
but a lifetime ahead of
where I've been

these dreams of day
never cease to amaze me
these dreams of day
these dreams of day

some sort of relief

I lay in bed at night
eyes wide open
staring at nothing
listening to the swinging chain
that dangles from my ceiling fan
as the blades spin

wondering where the years went
and having to remind myself
to breathe every now and then

there's a burning in my gut
that tends to go along with it
not physical pain like an ulcer
but an uneasiness
similar to infatuation
that keeps me awake
that keeps me tossing and turning

amusement has become
too difficult
I can't watch television anymore
I can't listen to the radio anymore
the internet makes me sick
and people are intolerable

there's a tragedy here
I just don't want to admit it
and there's nothing I can do
except head to the bar
to sit on a wobbly barstool
and drink myself stupid
and pray to a god
that I don't even believe in
for some sort of relief

I wonder if I'll ever get it

my misery

my misery always walks
a few steps behind me
waiting for the perfect moment
to leap onto my shoulders

so I write songs and perform at nightclubs
hoping to shake the vice like grip
it has upon me

my friends, my relations,
their friends, their relations
they crowd around
and take what little I have to give

with words and musical notes
I break open my chest
exposing my heart
my lungs
my spine
all for them to feast upon
to nourish their broken and damaged selves

I bare the pain with a smile
hoping that the gods
will reward my self sacrifice

but my misery is all too aware
and so it gains in its pursuit
the words take longer to write
the songs take longer to finish
the flesh I offer no longer satisfies
and so I lay down my instruments
I lay down my life
no longer seeing the greater good
all that was once a driving force
has diminished into a memory
softly, the notes begin to buzz
my misery no longer needs to chase me
my misery has been with me all along

last to know

I wish I had known
that it would be the last time
I'd kiss her

I wish I had known
that she was ready to say goodbye

I wish I had known
that in her mind
this day was imminent

I wish I had known

I would have kissed
her longer than I did

how I do it

people often ask me
"why don't you ever write about
happy things?"

my reply is always the same
"I don't know, that's just how
it comes out."

it's normally people who don't
know much about me that ask
and sometimes it's people who
think that they know something
about me that ask

but I could really give a shit
either way
I don't force it out
I let nature takes its course
it comes out how it comes out
and that's all there is to it

the brightest star

the bluish sky
turned reddish black

the day it lost
it's brightest star

to earth she came
and filled my days

with smiles
where sadness
used to stay

at times I'd wonder
why the sky
would cry
so fierce and feverishly

without a doubt
it knew the truth

that one day
she would be with me

corazón

I remember the song
that was playing
when I met you

I remember the song
that was playing
when you left

songs
make everything better
you see

songs
made you mean
the world to me

all of my heroes are dead

all of my heroes are dead
drinkers
drug addicts
liars
womanizers
losers
psychopaths
and so much more

all of my heroes are dead
laughing stocks
wimps
weirdos
anything bad that you can think of
in the mind of a mere mortal
who never ventured anything in life

all of my heroes broke free somehow
from the pain
from the regret
from the humiliation
of feeling feelings

all of my heroes rose above the ashes
of the taunts
of the heartache
of the ridicule
of the worry

all of my heroes soared into the sky
like phoenixes
becoming one with the gods
and breaking the shackles of their lesser selves

all of my heroes are dead
but only physically
they are alive through me
through my words
through my thoughts
through my actions
hopefully, I will live on
somehow, in some way
through the words of the next
through their emotions
through their up hill battles
through their pain
through their aggravations

and with that simple thought
I will lay my head upon my pillow
and sleep the sleep
of the damned

well, shit

broke, old, drunk
and lonely

lonely, old, broke
and drunk

no one calling
no one knocking
no one left
to argue with

sad, mad, confused
and petty

petty, mad, sad
and dumb

no one left to hear
my bullshit
no one left
to make me stop

face down, vomit
empty bottles

one shoe, lights on
brand new day

my own reflection
wants to leave me

crack the seal
and drink away

the night

the troubling thoughts
the creative ideas
the wild fantasies
they always come at night
when everything is quiet
when I have to get up
early the next day

the troubling thoughts
the creative ideas
the wild fantasies
they keep me awake
and the harder I try
to push them down
the harder I try to fall asleep
the deeper they dig in with
their claws

the troubling thoughts
the creative ideas
the wild fantasies
they don't care that
the sun will be up soon
they don't care that I'm
so very tired
they don't care that I'm trying
to do this sober

the troubling thoughts
the creative ideas
the wild fantasies
perhaps they're trying to
tell me something

shallow breathing

I sometimes wish

I could live in your imagination

I bet things would be
a lot easier there

we could finally do
whatever we wanted

let's get out of this place

are you ready

hillsides

the day burned bright
like a fiery hillside
caught off guard
to evil men

bestowed upon this
wicked world
were angels whistling
in the wind

eroded dreams
bled from the sky
entombing all within
their reach

as sadness choked
the impure air
where demons nest
to feed their young

impossible

funny, fake motherfuckers
everywhere I turn
I don't even have to aim
to hit them
fish in a fucking barrel

but how would I know
how would I realize
if and when
I started to become like them

here I sit in a trendy bar
surrounded by trendy music
and beautiful people

I have to admit
I don't feel so out of place
at least not as much
as I thought I would

could it be that I've been like them
all along
could it be that I'm a lame
funny, fake motherfucker too

impossible
there's no fucking way

hell is in my driveway

living on half a dream
while wasting time and money

talking to nobody
and thinking about everything

planning for something
that probably won't happen

the nights are hard and unforgiving
the nights are quiet, which makes them worse

most of the time
it's easier for me to sleep
when the sun is out
I wish that it wasn't like that for me

I really wish that I had mastered
the way of things
I really wish that I had mastered
the way of at least one thing

but I've wasted too much time
and now there's not enough left

hell is in my driveway
with the motor running
no time to even change my shirt
I'd better hurry before it starts to honk the horn

art and the cliché

art
what does it mean
what is it for
I suppose that it depends on the type of art
I like it all
but for me
music is the best
there's nothing quite like it
in the known universe

yet I
I am a cliché
I write poetry in dark bars
while drinking alone

I tend to feel rather silly about it
most of the time

it really isn't fair
that the writers who came before me
completely monopolized this scene

but what can I do about it

nothing

and if in a city with so much action
so many people
and so many lights and sounds
a person can still feel lost and lonely
I suppose it makes no real difference
whether I'm a cliché or not

because nobody is looking my way
I doubt that anyone
is paying any attention
at all

the noose in my back pocket

there were times
when I found it difficult to breathe

there were times
when I'd get a little bit dizzy

for a while there
I thought I was sick

but then I realized
that it only happened
in awkward or uncomfortable situations

and so I learned to stay away
from those situations

but then every situation
became one of those situations

and at that point I was fucked

nowhere to run
nowhere to hide

so now, I write
keeping the noose
in my back pocket
just in case

choices

the drinks kept coming
and I should've known better

when you're up
they want you down
when you're down
they're happy

it's god's way of giving you the finger
reminding you
to not feel so good about yourself
when you finally start to

reminding you
that in front of every silver lining
there's a dark cloud

I woke up feeling bad
I'll go to bed feeling bad
tomorrow will be the same

I'm fine with that
what other choice
do I have

asleep

how long have I been sleeping

where is my smile
my sense of pride
my brain feels bruised and cold
and toward the dark
my thoughts are creeping

like stranded angels in the attic
scratching through the walls
into my frozen heart they're reaching

they long to free my better side
but all they're going to find
is that this soul is sadly weeping

it weeps for moments thrown away
like pages from a failed play
so carelessly with swift neglect
and all while I was sleeping

this heart still longs for yesterday
but all that I can do
is pray it stops
while I am sleeping

three in the morning

blue skies
white clouds
and green trees
I fucking hate them
how can there be so
much beauty when I
feel so bad

laughter
jokes
and barbecues
I fucking hate them
how can there be so much
joy when I've been
torn in half

children
volleyball
and birthday parties
I fucking hate them
how can there be so
much leisure when
my heart is racing

black skies
no sounds
three in the morning
it's about fucking time

to be alone

when I'm alone I feel good
solitude does not bother me
to most it is an absolute terror
those are the people I avoid
I do not enjoy parties
I do not enjoy festivals
to be alone, for me, is bliss
it is the only personality trait
inherited from my father
that I am grateful for
to live the way I live
to be the way I am
it takes balls
it takes confidence
it takes thick skin
because family and friends
they are quick to judge
because family and friends
they are quick to criticize
they will often offer assistance
only to throw it in your face
as soon as the opportunity
presents itself
and who needs that kind of love
who needs that kind of situation
the place where I stay
has little to no style

the place where I stay
has little to no soul
the place where I stay
is death row for a guy like me
yet here I am
but not for long
not for long

the stained glass window

it's somewhat amazing to me
that time spent
with the one you love
in any given situation
in any given place
at any given moment
can easily explode into an ugly
and emotional ordeal

sitting in front of the stained glass window
of the bar across the boulevard
of my overpriced hotel room
with no one, as usual
because she's mad at me
as usual

but this time
I really don't give a shit
if this time is really the end
so be it
I may not be happy alone
but I may be happier alone

and if waking up with an upset stomach
after dreaming about her all night
or climbing the walls for a week
trying to figure out who she's been banging

is the price I have to pay
for not wanting to pull my hair out
every other week or so
I'm fine with that

I've been through it before and survived
I've learned how to roll with the punches
I'll be alright
let's get this show on the road

the right time

I save a bullet for the right time
I save my best whiskey for the right time
I save my dollars for the right time
I save the best record in my record collection
for the right time

this sleeplessness is getting old
these poems are getting old
these women are getting old
I'm getting old

the fear is getting stronger
the days are growing colder
the nights are feeling longer
the walls are getting closer

the bullet with the drink
the dollar for the song
the tightening of the walls
the right moment for the right time

the right time
has finally arrived

it's a tragedy

it's a tragedy
to walk amongst the soulless
to know that around every corner
there is a new crop
of virtual adventurers

to be in a room full of people
who are all staring down
at little blue screens
communicating with other people
who aren't really there

commenting
liking
sharing
selfie-ing

we have become a population
of narcissistic blank heads
we have become slaves
to instant gratification

no longer thinking
no longer feeling
no longer experiencing
unless it's through the
soft blue glow
of a little blue screen

I pray for a plague
or anything that will end this
mass madness

maybe I should I.M. god
or send him a text
I'm sure I'd get him to respond
for once

house of straw

there are so many times
when nothing helps

no amount of booze
no amount of ass
no amount of praise
no amount of cheers

there are so many times
when nothing holds up the facade

no amount of photos
no amount of style
no amount of swagger
no amount of success

there are so many times
when nothing keeps the wolves out

no amount of boards
no amount of nails
no amount of smoke
no amount of fire

there are so many times
like this one, right now
when the house of straw
is being blown apart

riot (a drunken conversation)

blah blah blah blah
(police sirens and bottles breaking)

I dropped out of school
(YEAH!!!)

blah blah blah blah
(police sirens and bottles breaking)

and we would get so fucking wasted
(police sirens and bottles breaking)

blah blah blah blah
... so he hands me the keys and says:

"you're driving today."

inspired by: (you know who you are)

shadow people

they come at any time
day or night
so long as you are sleeping
or rather
so long as your body is sleeping

they are called shadow people
and for good reason
as they sneak into your very being
at will

they only awaken your mind
upon their arrival
and they know how to paralyze
your body from head to toe

they paralyze your body
not through fear
but through some other mechanism
although the fear of their presence
in itself
is also quite paralyzing

they toy with you
in any way they please

they can even make it
difficult for you to breathe
I'm confident
they are the reason
people die in their sleep

for they have held me down
many times
and obstructed my airflow
to the point of complete
desperation

there were times
when I was certain
I was a goner because of them
and each time this happened
I'd hear them laughing
and snickering very closely to my ear

perhaps they are my own demons
crawling up through my spine
and into my head
repaying me for all of the shitty things
I've done

perhaps they are
from some other dimension
a dimension of a karma bar

and each stupid thing I've done
each person I've hurt or wronged
each one of those horrible actions of mine
has been like a drink being placed on my karma tab

perhaps they are arriving more frequently now
to let me know
that it's time for me
to pay the bill

and so now

down

way down

deep down inside

I have this bad, bad feeling
that last call
is rapidly approaching

Lyrics

We Cried For Fun

love machine gun

come up to my room I want you over
throw your clothes on the floor
and take me down

he doesn't make you move
I do it better
I don't need to love you girl to make it true
whoa tonight
I want tonight
to feel so right

oh, love machine gun
shoot em' up baby make em' run
love machine gun
shoot em' up make em' run
all night tonight

kill me softly girl but do it slower
throw yourself on the floor
and take me down

you don't need to love me girl
to do it better
I don't need to love you girl to make it true
whoa tonight
I want tonight
to feel so right
just shoot em' up

love machine gun
shoot em' up baby make em' run
love machine gun
shoot em' up make em' run
all night tonight

c'mon shoot em' up tonight now baby
shoot em' up tonight now baby

sedatives

give me one good reason why I
shouldn't want to buy my
sweet life saving sedatives

it's my one true heart's desire to
want to play with fire cause
life is so repetitive

when it's in my veins I find
I can leave it all behind
nothing else can make me feel this way
quickly day becomes the night
shaking and not feeling right
searching for the perfect words to say

I'm holding on to glimpses of a memory
that I used to own
if I could start this whole thing over
I would end it all alone

we've been harboring in style these
feelings of denial that
things will be alright again

but it's much easier to say we're
happier this way when hope has been forsaken

lost and covered in the mire
dancing in the devil's fire
drifting through a never ending maze
waiting for someone to say
things are going to be ok
trying to make it through another day

I'm holding on to glimpses of a memory
that I used to own
if I could start this whole thing over
I would end it all alone

with you

how can I
make you understand that
I just want to be with you

days go by
slowly oh so slowly
and I don't know what to do

my friends say I shouldn't waste my time
searching for a love I'll never find
but they
they just don't know you like I do
that's why I can't stop loving you

twiddle my thumbs
and watch the world go by
feeling completely hopeless
whoa, why do I do
the stupid things I do
to be with you

sentimental feelings all the time
such a shame that you were never mine
and now
you're moving on to something new
oh please don't take my heart
with you

love of mine

love of mine

won't you help
me understand
what's on your mind
this time

it's a crime
to mistreat
the one who
lives to make you smile
be kind

wonder

all alone I sit and wonder
where you are tonight

do the arms around you love you
just as much as mine

is it reasonable to say that
once our love was true

and that we had fun doing the things
we used to do

was there anything I could have said
to make you stay
was there anything I could have done

every now and then I pray for
life to go away
when I think of how you've really gone

all alone I'm wondering if you're
thinking of me too

has another done for you
what I could never do

when the morning comes
I pray the sun will go away

it can never bring you back
to me like yesterday

was there anything I could have said
to make you stay
was there anything I could have done

electrolight

thinking of the life I had before
staring blankly at the bedroom door
something in my heart won't let it go
I can't stop this feeling anymore

wheels are in motion now
wheels are in motion

staring at her shadow on the floor
the flowers in her hair begin to grow
something whispers to me from below
it won't rain forever anymore

wheels are in motion now
wheels are in motion

when I was lost in your eyes
it was so hard to disguise
all that I wanted to say

how did it end up this way

the breeze

I killed my love
I held her close under water
two steps above
my empty head
where I saw her

burned like the Sun
her cigarette on my shoulder
we cried for fun
so many times
when I told her

I pray to be
I pray to be
taken far away
I pray to be
I pray to be
taken far away
oh with the breeze

complaint

it's all over
they'll be coming for you now
gentle soldier
will you ever tell us how
they have thrown you
toward the sun

mock the spiders in the trees
with your confession
mock the spiders in the trees
with your confession

paper soldier
it's a shame to see you now
through the torture
speak the words that they'll allow
like the fire
of a gun

mock the spiders in the trees
with your confession
mock the spiders in the trees
with your confession

clovis

can I ask you a question
is there room in the house of detention
I hope it's not too late
for a fool far in need of redemption
and oh how my heart aches

there's a light shining bright in the corner
it's burning up the day
and the life that we led brought disorder
it's getting shorter

I'm a prisoner of consequence
as I secretly forget to notice
they're not forcing my captivity
it's my own desire
to keep from ever getting free

from all the pain, the choices made
there's not much left to say
I can't ignore, they're at the door
and they won't go away
no compromise to my surprise
there's nowhere left to climb
the tide is high, we must decide
to run for cover

I'm a prisoner of consequence
as I secretly forget to notice
they're not forcing my captivity
it's my own desire
to keep from getting free
until these words have bled from me, entirely

can I ask you a question
is there room in the house of detention
I hope it's not too late
for a fool far in need of redemption
my soul I hope he'll take

fed up

there's no time for us we're done
I can't wait to see you go

so much for grasping at the wings
of that elusive dream

I must do this alone

be free
there's no words for you to comfort me
be free
when I'm shining then maybe you'll see
so be free

things seemed perfect yesterday
we had the world on a string

but now you're folding to a life
of pure complacency

I must send you away

be free
there's no words for you to comfort me
be free
when I'm shining then maybe you'll see
so be free
go be free

Cut To Fit

midline

it's just another way to say
that times are changing again
please hold on to what tomorrow brings
and I'll be waiting
till then

just keep on singing that song
we loved for so long
maybe next time we'll have a chance to grow
it's not a lack of conversation
that made it so
hard to let you go

I love you so
it's been a fog of contemplation
but now I know

it's so hard to make it through the days
when I'm still waiting in vain
now I hear you're with somebody new
my dreams are fading away

so please keep singing that song we loved for so long
maybe next time we'll have a chance to grow
always remember there's someone out here
who loved you so
that they'd let you go

I hope you know
there'll always be somebody out here
who loves you so

there'll always be somebody out here
who loves you so

ghosts

I never meant to make you fall
I never meant to lead you on so long

if I knew what I'd become
I'd never make you come along
ooooh

I never meant to cause alarm
I never meant to cause you so much harm

if I knew what I'd become
I'd never make you come along

last to know

so many times
I'd let my feelings show
to my surprise
she was the last to know
I couldn't tell her
that I loved her so
that when I rise
she's where I want to go

is there no one
who will save me now

and now I find
another at her door
fresh out of time
I was the last to know
I should've told her
now she's gone for sure
I'll have to try
to carry on alone

is there no one
who will save me now

and now I find
another at her door
fresh out of time

I was the last to know
I should've told her
now she's gone for sure
I'll have to try
to carry on alone

is there no one
who will save me now

the bridge

run, tomorrow's gone
tomorrow run
tomorrow's gone
tomorrow's gone
gone

run, tomorrow's gone
tomorrow run
tomorrow's gone
tomorrow's gone
gone

sing my song
I know I always
sing the same old song
but now I'm done
done

I tried to try
tomorrow's gone
and I don't care
if all my friends
should cry
the sun no longer shines
and I just want to fly

had some fun
but now we're done
we had some fun
but now our time is done

I tried to try
tomorrow's gone
and I don't care
if all my friends
should cry
the sun no longer shines
and I just want to fly

french train

looking to the sky for help
but no one's out there
bleeding underneath the sun
I'm on my own

they don't even care to know my name, yeah
they don't even care to know my game, yeah
sing your list of last regrets to the unknown
don't want to hear about it

looking for a way to find that door to nowhere
bought my ticket for the train
it's time to go

they don't even care to know my pain, yeah
they don't even care to know my shame, yeah
sing your list of last regrets to the unknown
don't want to hear about it

there's no telling what we're in for
on this crazy ride uncontrolled
call my lover on a pay phone
tell my story on this train home

looking to the sky for help
but no one's out there
bleeding underneath the sun
I'm on my own

they don't even care to know my name, yeah
they don't even care to know my pain, yeah
sing your list of last regrets to the unknown
don't want to hear about it

there's no telling what we're in for
on this crazy ride uncontrolled
call my lover on a pay phone
tell my story on this train home, ooooh

the first one

dreamer
deceiver
you know I'm not awake

spoken
joking
you only come to take

but if I had the chance again
oooh I'd never let it end
how I wish this day was done
thinking of the only one who
broke my heart and made me cry
with the same old alibi
how I wish this day would end
wondering where my only friend has gone

laying
playing
it's getting hard to fake

seeing
believing
be real for heaven's sake

but if I had the chance again
oooh I'd never let it end

how I wish this day was done
thinking of the only one who
broke my heart and made me cry
with the same old alibi
how I wish this day would end
wondering where my only friend has gone

you're always on my mind
and even though I hate having you on my mind
I know there's no way I'll ever be able to get you
off of my mind

but if I had the chance again
oooh I'd never let it end
how I wish this day was done
thinking of the only one who
broke my heart and made me cry
with the same old alibi
how I wish this day would end
wondering where my only friend has gone

Bright Lights City

world outside

to the world outside
I say goodbye
to the world outside
I say goodbye
in a dreamers daze
my heart regrets
in a dreamers daze
my heart forgets

dream of summer
lovely lover
dream of summer
lovely lover

to the world outside
I say goodbye
to the world outside
I say goodbye
on a winter's day
my love confessed
on a winter's day
love laid to rest

dream of summer
lovely lover
dream of summer
lovely lover

3 A.M.

indiscriminate little woman
don't call my home
indiscriminate little woman
leave me alone
at 3 A.M. she's gone
at 3 A.M. she's calm
indiscriminate little woman
I called my own

ooh she's going to make you beg
ooh she'll get inside your head
ooh I want to make her dead
ooh the lies she spreads won't stop
until she meets her end

indiscriminate little woman
your smile is gone
indiscriminate little woman
your time has come
your wicked ways are done
there's nowhere left to run
indiscriminate little woman
who's had her fun

ooh she's going to make you beg
ooh she'll get inside your head
ooh I want to make her dead
ooh the lies she spreads won't stop
until she meets her end

friend to follow

friend to follow me home
going my way alone
my ways are old
their eyes are cold
need somebody to hold

I need a friend to follow
friend to follow
friend to follow me home
I need a friend to follow
friend to follow
friend to follow me home again

tried to change it with time
drowned in whiskey and wine
but no one knows
the pain that glows
down below the neon sign

I need a friend to follow
friend to follow
friend to follow me home
I need a friend to follow
friend to follow
friend to follow me home again, ooooh

break myself and fall to pieces
drown myself in the neon light
break myself and fall to pieces
drown myself tonight

I need a friend to follow
friend to follow
friend to follow me home
I need a friend to follow
friend to follow
friend to follow me home again, ooooh

bright lights city

bright lights city
I need someone to borrow
street walking woman
I've got some love to share
anywhere you go
I'm sure to follow
bright lights city
you caught me unaware
so unaware

sinful city
you make me feel so hollow
just for a little bit
I would like to care
such pretentious words
they'll make you swallow
bright lights city
your scars are ours to bare
all ours to bare

bright lights city
bright lights city

I'm a boy in need of love
she's the one I'm thinking of

dig me up

the television makes
my eyes turn red
my intuition burns
inside my head
these walls are closing in
I can't breathe quite right
if I don't find relief
I'm going to take my life tonight
somebody dig me up

the mirror image of
the filthy life I've led
stares like a thousand eyes
at the moments that I dread
somebody break me out
of this prison I invent
my love don't want me now
so I'll take a friend instead
she's going to dig me up

these scenes are black and white
and I feel I should be dead
nothing will satisfy
the body in my bed
I have no motivation to
bring me to the end
so tell the motivator
I chose the lead instead
nobody dug me up

Delete You After

delete you after

cynical disposition in my heart
there's no return, no need to start
cynical disposition in my heart
there's no return, no need to start

so we run, we run
and all our hopes, they lead us nowhere
run, we run
and all our hopes, they lead us nowhere

cynical ways to break it all apart
with every word, with any thought
cynical ways to break it all apart
with every word, with any thought

so we run, we run
and all our hopes, they lead us nowhere
run, we run
and all our hopes, they lead us nowhere

we run and all our hopes, they lead us nowhere now
we run and all our hopes, they lead us down

so we run, we run
and all our hopes, they lead us nowhere
run, we run
and all our hopes, they lead us nowhere
now

around the sun

terrorize the mind
realizing that we're fine
there's nowhere to find
a better place to hide, hide, hide
fearful of the tide
fearful of the softer side
where dreams often die
beneath a desperation sky, yea

oh... oh, follow us around the sun
follow us around the sun, yea
oh... oh, follow us around the sun
follow us around the sun, yea

following the blind
following the wrong design
we sway in the fire
with nothing left to find, find, find
waiting for the time
waiting for the light to shine
we pray for the lie
beneath a desperation sky, yea

oh... oh, follow us around the sun
follow us around the sun, yea
oh... oh, follow us around the sun
follow us around the sun, yea

realize the signs, of a desperation sky
realize the signs, of a desperation sky
in all who've seen them

oh... oh, follow us around the sun
follow us around the sun, yea
oh... oh, follow us around the sun
follow us around the sun, yea

we are

in a little place inside your mind
we will find the time
to finally unwind
in a little place we'll try to climb
never to remind
the ones we left behind

breathing out we are
we are, we are
breathing out we are

in a little place behind your eyes
love was our disguise
though it's of no surprise
so we never had to realize
hearts could not survive
within the walls we prized

breathing out we are
we are, we are
breathing out we are

bend it slowly
until the end of time
so I'll be the one
who's on your mind
this time

breathing out we are
we are, we are
breathing out we are

songs

songs play on the radio
I see you walking slowly
by the window all alone
songs may open up a door
to when you saw me smiling
by the dance floor long ago

save me something for tomorrow
I'll be home just waiting by the phone
save me something for tomorrow
I'll be home just waiting by the phone
waiting for you

songs we never cared to know
are playing through the speakers
of your bedroom stereo
songs we loved to sing before
may bring you dancing to me
like they did so long ago

save me something for tomorrow
I'll be home just waiting by the phone
save me something for tomorrow
I'll be home just waiting by the phone
waiting for you

stay with me, please don't fade away
stay with me, please don't fade away

save me something for tomorrow
I'll be home just waiting by the phone
save me something for tomorrow
I'll be home just waiting by the phone
waiting for you

out of control

let me whisper to you softly I can tell by the way
you roll your eyes there's something going on
lies have gotten far too easy and the truth is
something
I know I no longer can ignore

go before the night
crashes down around
the things we've tried to hide
it's all over baby
it's our life that's out of control
it's our life that's out of control
you got it

hide that smile that tends to please me
there's a life that's oh so complicating
waiting at the door
good time weather's always changing
and the blood inside our veins
is fading and begins to pour

though we tried to find ways to justify
the things we tried to hide
it's all over baby
it's our life that's out of control
it's our life that's out of control
you got it

I tell you baby
we're going to lose control
already knowing we've got nowhere to go
let me whisper to you softly
I can tell by the way you roll your eyes
there's something going on
already gone, it's all over baby

it's our life that's out of control
it's our life that's out of control
you got it

Vida

it's alright

you say you want to be my girl
you say you want to be my girl
but in the middle of the daytime
flying high
you tell me that it's alright
with just a little at the right time
slow inside
you tell me that it's alright
that it's alright

you say you want to be my girl
you say you want to be my girl
just like a fire in the night-time
shining bright
you tell me that it's alright
and with a burning up a lifetime
state of mind
you tell me that it's alright
that it's alright

bring it to me by the street sign
bring it to me all of the time
                    it's just a little at the right time
                    slow inside
bring it to me by the street sign
bring it to me all the time

cause it's alright

cause in the middle of the daytime
flying high
you told me that it's alright

>   *it's just a little at the right time*
>   *slow inside*

and with a burning up a lifetime
state of mind
you told me that it was time

sorrow

so we finally found our way back home
we wait for no one now
slowly our timing drowned us in the know
we wait for no one else now

we fell into their sorrow
we fell into their sorrow now

bleeding for the liars we have known
we wait for no one now
freedom we found it calmly on our own
we wait for no one else now

we fell into their sorrow
we fell into their sorrow now
rarely you're the one
finding peace of mind
in the sun

rarely you're the one
finding peace of mind
in the love we found now

we fell into their sorrow
we fell into their sorrow now

in my eyes

time moves slower
than water from my eyes
pride sinks lower and colder
from your lies

it's over
it's over now
it's over
in my eyes

fools and lovers
no others on their mind
lost and sober
no shoulder for your cries

it's over
it's over now
it's over
in my eyes

time flies so high
through my mind to the sky
time flies so high
through my mind to the sky

it's over
it's over now
it's over
in my eyes

now you're gone

so here we go again my love
it seems that we've been holding on to something
wrong
your actions say our time has come
the promises we made are done and now it's gone

oh how I wish that I had stayed
wish that I had changed it all
(wish that I had changed it all, wish that I had
changed)
oh how I wish that I had stayed
wish that I had changed

so here we go again my love
the same old situation and we don't belong
the light behind your eyes is lost
my callous heart won't pay the cost for anyone

oh how I wish that I had stayed
wish that I had changed it all
(wish that I had changed it all, wish that I had
changed)
oh how I wish that I had stayed
wish that I had changed
but it's too late cause now you're gone

oh how I wish that I had stayed
wish that I had changed it all
(wish that I had changed it all, wish that I had
changed)
oh how I wish that I had stayed
wish that I had changed
but it's too late cause now you're gone
but it's too late cause now you're gone
but it's too late cause now you're gone
but it's too late cause now you're gone
but it's too late cause now you're gone

vida

encantada con la pena de ayer
sonrisas en la sombra
que le consigue

santa, vida, fría, mía
santa, vida, fría, mi amor

entre la llamarada
tiempo se nos fue
perdidos en locura
que se puede hacer

santa, vida, fría, mía
santa, vida, fría, mi amor

encantada con ayer
encantada con ayer
encantada con ayer
encantada con ayer

santa, vida, fría, mia
santa, vida, fría, mi amor

mi amor

come around

there's a place for us
when we feel down and out
no tears or love songs
just three cheers all around

breathe out and smile again
the world will come around
hold on for one more day
the world will come around
ooooh

there's a place for us
where worry can't be found
no need for no one
just three cheers all around

breathe out and smile again
the world will come around
hold on for one more day
the world will come around
ooooh

holding on for one more day
the world is ours
hold on for one more day
the world is ours

breathe out and smile again
the world will come around
hold on for one more day
the world will come around
ooooh

Truth By Moonlight

ordinary day

just a call away
ordinary day

loneliness is just a call away
phoning for an ordinary day
the silence on the other end
it brings me to my knees
dying from a broken heart disease
so I say

I don't want to fall in love again
I don't want to be the one again
I don't want to fall in love again
I don't want to be the one
whose compromises signify the end

trade my voice to pass the time away
finding that I've nothing left to say
the wind, it blows inside my room
and takes my breath away
softer than the loss that's here to stay
so I say

I don't want to fall in love again
I don't want to be the one again
I don't want to fall in love again
I don't want to be the one
whose compromises signify the end

loneliness is just a call away
loneliness is just a call away
loneliness is just a call away
loneliness is just a call away
loneliness is just a call away

killer at the door

trying to find the cause of this disaster
waiting for the calm before the storm
wasting time on things that just don't matter
sinking faster than I have before

searching for the answers getting nowhere
sifting through the cracks along the floor
searching for the answers getting nowhere
hoping there's a killer at the door

still while everything keeps moving faster
drifting like the ship's out of control
loss of satisfaction while I'm sober
slipping faster than I have before

searching for the answers getting nowhere
sifting through the cracks along the floor
searching for the answers getting nowhere
hoping there's a killer at the door
hoping there's a killer at the door

searching for the answers getting nowhere
sifting through the cracks along the floor
searching for the answers getting nowhere
hoping there's a killer at the door
hoping there's a killer at the door
hoping there's a killer at the door

break me out

0, 0, 9, 6, 2, 2, 5, 1, 2, 1, 1, 0, 0, 0, 2, 1...

tell them not to show who's left
time is moving slow again

break me out
break me out
break me out
break me out, ooooooooooooooooooooo......

friends I used to know are dead
flown over the edge instead

break me out
break me out
break me out
break me out, ooooooooooooooooooooo......

0, 0, 9, 6, 2, 2, 5, 1, 2, 1, 1, 0, 0, 0, 2, 1...

friends I used to know are dead
time is moving slow again

break me out
break me out
break me out
break me out, ooooooooooooooooooooo......

political disco

the glowing lights of our computer screens burning
through our eyes
inner intelligence asks, what's it all for
the flashing lights upon our TV screens beaming us
the lies
we need to ask ourselves, what's it all for

we need to ask ourselves, what's it all for
we need to ask ourselves, what's it all for
we need to ask ourselves, what's it all for
we need to ask ourselves, what's it all for

the fight or flight of our biology seems to override
our best technology, what's it all for
the story of our faux democracy, history and lies
are so we never wonder, what's it all for

it's so we never wonder, what's it all for
it's so we never wonder, what's it all for
it's so we never wonder, what's it all for
it's so we never wonder, what's it all for

the lessons of our lost economy, guns and drugs and
crime
escape the symbol minded, what's it all for
the structure of pre-destined poverty, leads to the
demise
of our society, what's it all for

so called society, what's it all for
so called society, what's it all for
so called society, what's it all for
so called society, what's it all for

CPSIA information can be obtained
at www.ICGtesting.com
Printed in the USA
BVHW071953300122
627572BV00005B/218